BIBLE BRAIN QUEST®

FOR KIDS

HARVEST HOUSE PUBLISHERS
EUGENE, OREGON

Scripture references in *Bible Brain Quest*® are based on...

the Holy Bible, New International Version®, NIV®. Copyright © 1973, 1978, 1984, 2011 by Biblica, Inc.® Used by permission. All rights reserved worldwide.

the King James Version of the Bible

Questions and Answers by Dan Penwell

Illustrations by Matt Rockefeller

Cover design by Kyler Dougherty

BRAIN QUEST is a registered trademark of Workman Publishing Company, Inc.

BIBLE BRAIN QUEST® FOR KIDS

Copyright © 2017 by Workman Publishing Co., Inc.
Published by Harvest House Publishers
Eugene, Oregon 97402
www.harvesthousepublishers.com
Published under license with Workman Publishing Co., Inc.

ISBN 978-0-7369-6882-9 (pbk.)
ISBN 978-0-7369-6883-6 (eBook)

Printed in the United States of America

17 18 19 20 21 22 23 24 25 / VP-JC / 10 9 8 7 6 5 4 3 2 1

Suggested Ways to Keep Score

The 10-Point Game

Each player or team takes turns asking questions. Correct answers are worth 1 point. (Genius answers, indicated by GENIUS, are worth 2 points). The first player or team to score 10 points wins!

The 5-Minute Game

Each player or team takes turns firing questions at an opponent for 5 minutes. Whoever scores highest in the 5-minute period wins!

Solitaire

Answer each question on a page and then check your answers on the next page. Your quest? To get them all right!

Contents

The Beginning of the World

1. Arrange these books of the Bible in the proper order: Deuteronomy, Leviticus, Exodus, Numbers, Genesis.

2. What are the first three words of the Old Testament?

3. How many days did it take God to create the world?

4. Which appeared first on earth during the period of creation: light, plants, or animals?

5. Name the three great lights that God created for day and night.

6. On what day of creation did God make Adam?

7. In whose image did God create human beings?

1

The Beginning of the World

1. Genesis, Exodus, Leviticus, Numbers, Deuteronomy (the books of Moses)

2. "In the beginning…"

3. six days (God blessed the seventh day, on which He rested, and made it holy.)

4. light (God then separated the light from the darkness to make day and night.)

5. the sun, the moon and the stars (on the fourth day of creation)

6. the sixth day (God rested on the seventh day.)

7. in His own image

8. How did Adam receive the breath of life?

9. What bone did God take from Adam's side to create Eve?

GENIUS

10. According to Genesis, where did God place the tree of life?

11. Adam took care of all the plants in the Garden of Eden. Who was his helper?

12. Adam and Eve were forbidden to eat the fruit of which tree in the Garden of Eden?

13. Which tree is mentioned first in the Bible: the tree of life or the tree of the knowledge of good and evil?

14. In the Garden of Eden, did Satan appear to Eve as a toad, a serpent, or a dragon?

GENIUS

8. God breathed into Adam's nostrils (and man became a human being).

9. a rib (God put Adam into a deep sleep in order to create Eve.)

10. in the middle of the Garden of Eden (where the tree of the knowledge of good and evil also stood)

11. Eve, his wife (Their story is told in Genesis, the first book of the Bible.)

12. the tree of the knowledge of good and evil

13. the tree of life

14. a serpent (or snake)

15. Who offered Adam the forbidden fruit in the Garden of Eden?

16. Adam and Eve made their first clothing out of animal skins. True or false?

17. When God asked where Abel was, who answered with the words: "Am I my brother's keeper?"

GENIUS

18. Was Adam or Cain banished to a place that lay to the east of Eden?

19. Was the third son of Adam and Eve named Seth or Shem?

20. What righteous man did God remember when He decided to destroy all the people and animals?

GENIUS

21. Was Noah the grandson of Methuselah or Obed?

15. Eve (after the serpent had persuaded her to eat some herself)

16. false (They made their first clothing out of fig leaves.)

17. Cain (who had slain Abel, his younger brother)

GENIUS

18. Cain (God condemned him to a lifetime of wandering for having murdered his brother Abel.)

19. Seth (Shem was the eldest son of Noah.)

20. Noah (God told Noah to build an ark because floodwaters would cover the earth.)

GENIUS

21. Methuselah (who lived for 969 years, longer than any other biblical figure)

22. In the days of Noah, why did God bring a great flood on the whole world?

GENIUS

23. How many people were passengers on the ark that Noah built?

24. How long did God make it rain during the flood in the days of Noah?

25. While Noah was on the ark, the floodwaters rose about twenty feet above the mountaintops. True or false?

GENIUS

26. Name one of the two birds that Noah sent from the ark.

GENIUS

27. Was an olive leaf brought to Noah's ark in the mouth of the raven or the dove?

28. Where did Noah's ark come to rest after the flood?

GENIUS

22. because the people of the world had become very evil

23. eight (Noah, his wife, his three sons and their wives)

24. forty days and forty nights

25. true (Every land creature and bird outside the ark perished during the flood.)

GENIUS

26. a raven and a dove

GENIUS

27. the dove (Noah knew then that the water had receded from the earth.)

28. on Mount Ararat (in present-day Turkey)

29. What did God place in the heavens as a symbol of His pledge to Noah and his family?

30. Was Noah the first man to plant a vineyard or to build a chariot?

31. What materials were used to build the Tower of Babel?

29. a rainbow (God promised that He would never again destroy the earth with a great flood.)

30. to plant a vineyard

31. bricks (with tar for mortar)

The Patriarchs

1. Who was the first great ancestor of the people of Israel?

2. Abraham was born in Ur. Was this ancient city in Mesopotamia or Egypt?

3. After leaving Ur, did Abraham move to Canaan or to Sodom?

4. Did Abraham build a house for his family or an altar to the Lord near the town of Bethel?

5. Which woman was the wife of Abraham and the mother of Isaac: Sarah or Rebekah?

6. Was Sarah's Egyptian handmaid named Ruth or Hagar?

7. In the book of Genesis, who defeated the four kings who carried off his nephew?

2

The Patriarchs

1. Abraham (Isaac and Jacob were the second and third patriarchs.)

2. Mesopotamia

3. to Canaan (His nephew Lot moved to Sodom.)

4. an altar to the Lord (where he prayed before continuing on to Egypt)

5. Sarah (Rebekah was Isaac's wife.)

6. Hagar ("Handmaid" is another word for a servant.)

7. Abraham (His nephew Lot had been taken captive in the kingdom of Sodom.)

8. Who is the first person in the Bible to be called a Hebrew: Abraham, Isaac, or Jacob?

9. Did God destroy Sodom and Gomorrah by fire and brimstone or by rain and flood?

10. What happened to Lot's wife when she looked back at the burning city of Sodom?

11. Ishmael was the son of Hagar. Who was his father?

12. Who called to Abraham and stopped him from sacrificing his son Isaac?

GENIUS

13. What did Abraham's servant give Rebekah after she offered water to him and his camels?

GENIUS

14. Did Abraham purchase a cave for his family's tomb in Hebron, Shiloh, or Jerusalem?

15. When Isaac first saw Rebekah, was she riding on a camel or in a chariot?

8. Abraham (in Genesis 14, when he recues his nephew Lot)

9. by fire and brimstone

10. She turned into a pillar of salt.

11. Abraham (who was also the father of Isaac)

12. an angel

GENIUS

13. a golden earring and two bracelets

GENIUS

14. Hebron (Abraham bought the cave and the field around it from the Hittites.)

15. on a camel

16. Which twin sold his birthright to his brother: Esau or Jacob?

GENIUS

17. What animal skin did Jacob put on his hands and neck so his father would think he was hairy like Esau?

GENIUS

18. What did Jacob name the place where he dreamed of a ladder with angels going up and down?

GENIUS

19. Who took Jacob into his home after he stole Esau's blessing?

20. Who begged her sister Leah for mandrake plants, hoping they would help her bear children?

21. What new name did God give to Jacob?

22. Did Jacob raise his twelve sons in Moab, Canaan, or Ammon?

23. What celestial objects bowed down to Joseph in the dream he related to his family?

16. Esau (the firstborn twin son of Isaac)

17. goat skin (Jacob wanted to receive the blessing that belonged to his brother.)

18. Bethel (Jacob marked the place with the stone he had used as a pillow.)

19. Laban (Jacob's uncle, his mother's brother)

20. Rachel (Leah's eldest son, Reuben, had just brought them to his mother.)

21. Israel (after he wrestled with the angel)

22. Canaan (inhabited by the Canaanites until the conquest of the Israelites)

23. the sun, the moon, and eleven stars (which his father, Jacob, said symbolized his parents and eleven brothers)

24. What present from his father made Joseph's brothers turn against him?

25. Was Joseph's coat of many colors smeared with the blood of a goat or his own blood?

26. Joseph was the eleventh son born to Jacob. Who was the twelfth son?

27. In the book of Genesis, which city was called Ephrath: Jerusalem or Bethlehem?

28. Who became the slave of Potiphar, the captain of Pharaoh's guard?

29. Did young Joseph become an important ruler in Egypt, Samaria, or Rome?

30. In Pharaoh's dream, what animals represented prosperity and famine?

31. Joseph helped prepare Egypt for a great famine. What is a famine?

24. a coat of many colors (Joseph was Jacob's favorite son.)

25. the blood of a goat (so Jacob would think that it was Joseph's blood and that his son was dead)

26. Benjamin (the second son born to Rachel after her marriage to Jacob)

27. Bethlehem (which has been continuously inhabited for about thirty-three centuries)

28. Joseph (after his arrival in Egypt)

29. Egypt (where Joseph was sold into slavery by merchants who bought him from his brothers)

30. cows (In the dream interpreted by Joseph, seven sickly cows ate seven well-fed cows.)

31. a period of time when there is little or no food

GENIUS

32. Which of his brothers did Joseph put in jail: Levi, Simeon, or Judah?

33. Did Jacob's family settle in Goshen, Midian, or the Sinai desert when they went to Egypt to escape famine?

34. How many tribes or families came from Jacob's sons?

35. By what name did the family and descendants of Levi become known?

GENIUS

32. Simeon (until the other nine brothers returned with Benjamin, the youngest brother)

33. Goshen (The Israelites occupied this land from the time of Joseph until the exodus.)

34. twelve (the Twelve Tribes of Israel)

35. the Levites (Levi was the third son of Jacob and Leah.)

3

Israel Becomes a Nation

1. How many books of the Bible were written by Moses?

2. Was the older brother of Moses named Aaron, Joel or Jethro?

3. Which plant was used to make the basket for baby Moses: the bulrush or the palm tree?

4. Did Pharaoh's daughter find the baby Moses floating in a basket on the river Nile or the river Jordan?

5. Who was hired by Pharaoh's daughter to care for the baby Moses?

6. After killing an Egyptian taskmaster, did Moses flee to Canaan or Midian?

7. Was the wife of Moses named Zipporah or Gershom?

3

Israel Becomes a Nation

1. five (the first five books of the Old Testament)

2. Aaron (He joined Moses in asking Pharaoh to let their people leave Egypt.)

3. the bulrush (or the papyrus plant)

4. the river Nile (in Egypt)

5. Moses' real mother (who educated her son in the ways of the Israelites)

GENIUS

6. Midian

GENIUS

7. Zipporah (Gershom was Moses' first son.)

8. When God appeared in a burning bush, what article of clothing did He tell Moses to remove?

9. Moses watched as the burning bush was destroyed by flames. True or false?

10. God promised Moses that he would take the Israelites to a land of cream and sugar. True or false?

11. Who said, "I Am Who I Am"?

12. What happened to the rod that Aaron threw on the ground before Pharaoh?

13. During the first plague that God brought upon Egypt, what happened to all the water?

14. What small, four-legged green animals were one of the plagues upon Egypt?

15. In the third plague upon Egypt, were the people attacked by boils, gnats, or hail?

GENIUS

8. his sandals, or shoes (for Moses was standing on holy ground)

9. false (Miraculously, the bush did not burn up.)

10. false (Moses would take them to a land of milk and honey.)

11. God (when Moses asked Him how to answer the Israelites who wanted to know His name)

12. It turned into a serpent (or snake).

13. It turned to blood (and no one could drink it).

14. frogs (which went into the houses and even into Pharaoh's palace)

15. gnats (formed from the dust of the land)

GENIUS

16. The fourth plague that God brought on Egypt was a tremendous swarm of flies. True or false?

17. How many plagues in all did God bring upon Egypt?

18. In the Bible, how many of the children of Israel left Egypt for the Promised Land: 20,000 or 2,000,000?

GENIUS

19. Whose bones were carried in a coffin through the wilderness for forty years?

20. To help the Israelites escape their enemies, did God part the Red Sea or build a bridge over it?

21. What catastrophe awaited Pharaoh's soldiers when they chased the Israelites into the Red Sea?

22. What did God do to the wheels of the Egyptian chariots that were chasing Moses and the Israelites?

23. Where did the children of Israel wander for forty years after they left Egypt?

GENIUS

16. true (The first three plagues were blood, frogs and gnats.)

17. ten (blood, frogs, gnats, flies, dead livestock, boils, hail, locusts, darkness, death of firstborn sons)

18. 2,000,000

19. Joseph's bones (at his own request)

20. God parted the Red Sea (so the Israelites could cross to the other side).

21. They drowned (when God closed the waters over their heads).

22. God made them fall off (so the Egyptians had difficulty driving).

23. in the wilderness (or desert)

GENIUS

24. What was used to create the golden calf in the wilderness?

25. Moses made the Israelites drink a mixture prepared from the ashes of the golden calf. True or false?

26. What do we call the set of laws that Moses brought down from the mountain?

27. Did Moses receive the Ten Commandments on Mount Sinai or the Mount of Olives?

28. After his talk with God on Mount Sinai, was Moses' face radiant and shining or veiled and invisible?

29. Did God tell Moses to build an altar out of cut stones or uncut stones?

30. Which kind of wood was used for the Ark of the Covenant: Balsam, cedar, or acacia?

31. Complete this verse from the Ten Commandments: "You shall have no other gods _____."

24. the gold from earrings belonging to the Israelites' wives, daughters, and sons

25. true (Moses burned the golden calf, ground it into powder, and poured it into water.)

26. the Ten Commandments (inscribed on two stone tablets)

27. Mount Sinai (a mountain near the land known today as the Sinai Peninsula)

28. radiant and shining

29. uncut stones (because using a tool to cut the stones would defile the altar)

30. acacia (covered with gold)

31. before me

GENIUS

32. What is the Fifth Commandment?

33. Which one of the five books of Moses is filled mainly with rules, laws, and regulations?

34. In order to be considered clean, lepers had to shave their heads twice, six days apart. True or false?

35. Giving the "first fruits" to God meant offering the first part of one's crop. True or false?

36. What percent of their income were the Israelites expected to give back to God?

37. Which animal was unclean for the people of Israel to eat or sacrifice: the pig or the bull?

38. Which animal was NOT an acceptable sacrifice to God: a goat, a lamb, or a camel?

39. Did Jewish law permit a couple to enjoy a honeymoon for one week, one month, or one year?

GENIUS

32. Honor your father and mother.

33. the book of Leviticus (the third book of the Old Testament)

34. true (according to Leviticus 14)

35. true (The fruits of the first crop were dedicated to God.)

36. ten percent (A tenth of one's income was called a tithe.)

37. the pig (because pigs do not chew cud)

38. a camel (Although it chews cud, the camel does not have split hooves.)

39. one year (according to Deuteronomy 24:5)

40. Which is known as the Feast of Unleavened Bread: Passover or Pentecost?

41. Who was selected to be the chief priest of the tabernacle in the wilderness?

42. Was the one major responsibility of the Levites to be carpenters, priests, or military officials?

43. Did Aaron's staff miraculously change color or did it blossom and produce almonds?

44. What book of the Bible was named for the counting, or census, of the Israelites in the desert?

45. What did God use during the day to guide the Israelites through the wilderness?

46. What miraculous event occurred when Moses struck a rock in the wilderness?

47. What did the Israelites call the portable sacred tent they used for worship?

Answers

40. Passover (Pentecost occurs fifty days after the start of Passover.)

41. Aaron (a brother of Moses and a member of the tribe of Levi)

42. priests (and their helpers)

43. It blossomed and produced almonds (and served to put an end to the grumbling of the Israelites against God).

44. the book of Numbers (the fourth book of the Old Testament)

45. a pillar of cloud (or a column of smoke)

46. Water came out of the rock (so that the Israelites could drink).

47. the tabernacle (People went to this sacred tent to worship God.)

48. What food provided to the Israelites in the wilderness tasted like honey wafers?

49. What birds did God send in the evening as food for the Israelites in the wilderness?

50. Which brother did Miriam speak out against: Moses or Aaron?

51. What animals did God send to the Israelites when they spoke against Him and against Moses?

GENIUS

52. Whose donkey said, "What have I done to you to make you beat me three times"?

53. Moses never got to enter into the Promised Land. True or false?

54. Which book contains Moses' last words to the Israelites as they prepared to enter the Promised Land?

48. manna (according to Exodus 16:31)

49. quail (God provided manna in the morning.)

50. Moses (because he married a woman from Ethiopia)

51. poisonous snakes (which bit the Israelites and caused many of them to die)

52. Balaam's donkey (when she saw an angel blocking the road and didn't listen to her master)

53. true (God showed the Promised Land to Moses as he stood atop Mount Nebo.)

54. Deuteronomy (Named for a Greek word meaning "second law," this book adds to the laws of earlier books.)

GENIUS

In the Promised Land

1. What was the name of the land that was said to flow with milk and honey?

2. Of the Israelites twenty years of age or over, how many entered the Promised Land?

3. What happened to the river Jordan when the priests carrying the Ark of the Covenant stepped into it?

4. Name the city whose walls fell down when the trumpets blared and the Israelites shouted.

5. How many times did Joshua and his people march around the city of Jericho on the seventh day?

6. Who killed five kings and hanged them from five trees: Joshua or David?

7. What happened to the sun as the Israelites fought the Amorites?

4

In the Promised Land

GENIUS

1. Canaan

2. two (Joshua and Caleb)

3. The water divided, and the Israelites walked on dry ground to the Promised Land.

4. Jericho (the site of the Israelites' first victory in the Promised Land)

5. seven times

GENIUS

6. Joshua (during his conquests in Canaan)

7. It stood still (until the Israelites won the battle).

8. Of the twelve judges in the Old Testament, which one was a woman?

9. What well-known judge and Nazirite took a vow that included not allowing his hair to be cut?

10. Did Gideon test his men to find the best 300 warriors on a mountaintop or at the edge of a stream?

11. Who singlehandedly killed a thousand Philistines with a jawbone of a donkey?

12. The commotion by Gideon's 300 soldiers caused the men of Midian to fight and kill each other. True or false?

13. Name the Old Testament judge who told a fascinating riddle about honey.

14. Who finally tricked Samson into telling the secret of his strength?

15. Which one of the Twelve Tribes had 700 left-handed, sling-shot soldiers?

GENIUS

8. Deborah (whose achievements are celebrated in the book of Judges)

9. Samson (He would lose his strength if his hair was cut.)

10. at the edge of a stream

11. Samson (as vengeance on the Philistines)

12. true (The soldiers smashed their jars, blew their trumpets and raised their torches.)

13. Samson ("Out of the eater, something to eat; out of the strong, something sweet.")

14. Delilah (Samson told her that he would lose his strength if his hair was cut.)

15. the tribe of Benjamin (which fought the other tribes of Israel and lost on the third day)

GENIUS

GENIUS

16. Was Ruth from the country of Moab or Edom?

GENIUS

17. Did Ruth accompany Naomi to Jerusalem or Bethlehem?

18. Boaz and Ruth were the great-grandparents of David and the eventual ancestors of Jesus. True or false?

19. Who prayed to God to give her a son: Hannah, Naomi, or Deborah?

GENIUS

20. Who called to Samuel four times while he slept in the temple at Shiloh?

GENIUS

16. Moab (a region in present-day Jordan)

GENIUS

17. Bethlehem (Naomi, Ruth's mother-in-law, wanted to return home after her husband and sons died.)

18. true (Jesse, the father of David, was born to their son Obed.)

19. Hannah (Her son was Samuel, who became a prophet and a judge of the Israelites.)

GENIUS

20. God (From then on He spoke to Samuel, who became a prophet.)

The Kings of Israel

1. Who was NOT a king of Israel? Saul, David, Moses, Solomon?

2. Who was the first king of the Israelites?

3. Was King David's father named Obed, Samuel, or Jesse?

4. In the Old Testament, which king stood a head taller than his people: Saul, David, or Solomon?

5. When King Saul needed advice near the end of his life, did he first turn to God or the witch in Endor?

6. What musical instrument did David play?

7. What king was Samuel addressing when he said: "To obey is better than to sacrifice"?

GENIUS

The Kings of Israel

1. Moses (who led the Israelites out of Egypt)

2. Saul

3. Jesse (son of Obed)

4. Saul

5. to God (When God didn't answer, Saul turned to the witch in Endor.)

6. the harp (or lyre)

7. King Saul (who disobeyed God by not destroying everything that belonged to the Amalekites)

GENIUS

8. While protecting his sheep, the shepherd David killed a lion and a bear. True or false?

9. God was very pleased that he had selected Saul as the first king of Israel. True or false?

10. Was the giant Goliath born in Gath, Gaza, or Gilead?

11. How many smooth stones did David pick up at the riverbed before he fought the giant Goliath?

12. Who was King Saul's eldest son and David's closest friend?

13. King Saul's daughter became King David's wife. Was she named Michal, Esther, or Bathsheba?

14. Name the king who united the Israelite tribes of the north and the south.

15. On special occasions, did King David and King Solomon ride an elephant or a mule?

8. true (David believed that the Lord, who saved him from the lion and bear, would save him from Goliath.)

9. false (Saul was a good king at first, but he did not remain loyal and obedient to God.)

10. Gath (a city in Philistia)

11. five smooth stones

12. Jonathan (who once save David's life)

13. Michal (She helped David escape from her jealous father.)

14. King David (the second king of Israel)

15. a mule (regarded as a special animal and appropriate for royalty)

16. King David arranged for Bathsheba's husband to be killed in a battle. Was his name Uriah or Ulysses?

17. Was David's reaction at the death of King Saul one of extreme happiness or intense sadness?

18. Which prophet told a parable pointing out the sin of David with Bathsheba: Nathan or Samuel?

19. God refused to punish King David for his sin with Bathsheba. True or false?

20. Did God give King Solomon the gift of strength or the gift of wisdom?

21. How did King Solomon decide the case of the two women who both claimed the same son?

22. What was King Solomon known for besides his great wisdom?

23. King Solomon's Temple was approximately 90 feet long, 30 feet wide and 45 feet high. True or false?

GENIUS

16. Uriah (a Hittite who was loyal to David)

17. intense sadness (even though Saul had once tried to kill David)

18. Nathan (When David heard the story, he repented for his actions.)

19. false (God took their first son as punishment.)

20. the gift of wisdom

21. He instructed them to cut the child into two pieces (knowing the real mother would not let this happen).

22. his great wealth

23. true (The Temple is fully described in 1 Kings, chapter 6.)

GENIUS

24. How many men did King Solomon use in building the Temple in Jerusalem: 1,800, 18,000, or 180,000?

25. How many years did it take Solomon to build the Temple in Jerusalem: seven, nine, or thirteen?

26. Did the glory of the Lord or the smell of flowers fill the new Temple of God during its dedication?

27. Did King David or King Solomon build a naval fleet by the Red Sea?

28. Did a queen from Sheba or from Ammon come to meet King Solomon and seek his wisdom?

29. What animals did the ships of Tarshish bring to Solomon?

30. What two kingdoms are featured in First and Second Kings?

GENIUS

24. 180,000 men

25. seven years (Solomon spent thirteen years building his own palace.)

26. the glory of the Lord (in the form of a cloud)

27. King Solomon

28. a queen from Sheba

29. apes and peacocks (in addition to gold, silver, and ivory)

30. Israel and Judah

GENIUS

GENIUS

31. Was King Ahab's palace located in Jerusalem or Samaria?

GENIUS

32. At the death of Solomon, who inherited his kingdom: Rehoboam or Jeroboam?

33. Which queen plotted Naboth's death to get his land and to please her husband: Esther or Jezebel?

34. Which was the god of Jezebel: Baal, Ishtar, or Dagon?

35. What queen painted her face and arranged her hair to meet the new king of Israel?

GENIUS

36. Which city was the capital of Assyria: Babylon, Tyre, or Nineveh?

37. Did God add fifteen years to the life of King Hezekiah or King Zechariah?

GENIUS

31. Samaria (Ahab ruled over Israel from Samaria for twenty-two years.)

GENIUS

32. Rehoboam, his son (The kingdom split, and Jeroboam ruled the northern kingdom called Israel.)

33. Jezebel (the wife of King Ahab)

34. Baal (Ishtar was the god of the Assyrians; Dagon the god of the Philistines.)

35. Jezebel (She was a wicked queen who met her death when King Jehu had her thrown out a window.)

GENIUS

36. Nineveh (where Jonah was sent to preach against the people's sinful ways)

37. King Hezekiah (God heard his prayer not to die and also promised to save Jerusalem from the Assyrians.)

38. What seventy-five-foot structure did Haman build for Queen Esther's cousin Mordecai?

39. Who told Esther about Haman's plot against the Jews?

40. When Nehemiah returned to Jerusalem, did he rebuild the walls of the city or the Temple of the Lord?

41. What book did Ezra read to the Israelite exiles from daybreak to noon?

38. a gallows (on which to hang Mordecai)

39. Mordecai, Esther's cousin

40. the walls of the city (Despite great opposition, the work was completed in fifty-two days.)

41. the Book of the Law of Moses

Israel's Songs and Sayings

GENIUS   **1.** Who lost three thousand camels when God tested the limits of his faith?

GENIUS   **2.** To whom was God speaking when he said about Job: "He is in your hands, but you must spare his life"?

GENIUS   **3.** Who was killed in Job's family as the result of a great storm?

4. Who said in the midst of tragedy and misery, "Curse God, and die": Job's wife or Queen Jezebel?

5. Were Eliphaz, Bildad, and Zophar friends of Job or Samson?

6. Even though Job faced tremendous hardship and misery, he never uttered a sinful word. True or false?

7. Is a biblical song called a psalm or a proverb?

Israel's Songs and Sayings

1. Job (who regained his wealth after proving his faith despite his terrible misfortunes)

2. Satan (about the testing to come upon Job)

3. all of his sons and daughters

4. Job's wife (who believed her husband should forsake God)

5. Job (The three men tried to console and comfort him during his tests of faith.)

6. true (Job's faith in God was never shaken.)

7. a psalm (There are 150 psalms in the book of Psalms.)

8. The psalms were written to be sung with musical instruments. True or false?

9. All the psalms were written by King David. True or false?

10. Which psalm begins, "The Lord is my shepherd; I shall not want..."?

11. Did David say that human beings are a little higher than the animals or a little lower than the angels?

GENIUS

12. Which psalm is the longest in the Bible: 29, 119, or 127?

13. Who was the first person to describe plant life and teach about animals: Adam, David, or Solomon?

GENIUS

14. According to Proverbs 6, what tiny insect can teach us about hard work?

15. Does Proverbs 1 or Proverbs 31 talk about the characteristics of an honorable, worthy wife?

8. true

9. false (Most are by David, but Asaph and others wrote some of the psalms.)

10. the Twenty-Third Psalm (written by David)

11. a little lower than the angels

GENIUS

12. Psalm 119 (with 176 verses)

13. Solomon (People of all nations came to listen to him and learn from his wisdom.)

GENIUS

14. the ant (a model of industry and efficiency)

15. Proverbs 31

16. Do the words "Fear God and keep his command-ments" appear in Genesis or Ecclesiastes?

17. Finish this phrase from Ecclesiastes: "a time to be born and a time _____."

GENIUS

18. Does the Old Testament book Song of Songs tell a love story or a parable?

16. Ecclesiastes (thought to be written by King Solomon)

17. to die (one of the many seasonal times mentioned in chapter 3)

GENIUS

18. a love story (thought to be about Solomon's love for a young woman)

7

The Prophets

1. In the Old Testament, God sometimes performed his miracles through the prophets. True or false?

2. Did Elijah or Jesus stretch out on the dead son of the Shunammite woman and bring him back to life?

3. What miraculous food supply did Elijah provide for the poor widow of Zarephath?

4. What animal did Elijah and the prophets of Baal sacrifice in their contest on Mount Carmel?

5. In his contest with the prophets of Baal, what was poured on Elijah's sacrifice?

6. After the contest on Mount Carmel, did Elijah run after Ahab's chariot or before it?

7. Who was left behind on the ground when God took Elijah up to heaven in a fiery chariot?

7

The Prophets

1. true (Elijah and Elisha were two of the prophets chosen by God to perform His miracles.)

2. Elijah

3. oil and flour (which could never be used up)

4. Each sacrificed a bull.

5. water (which did not keep the sacrifice from burning up)

6. before it (all the way to Jezreel)

7. Elisha (a follower of Elijah who became his successor)

8. What garment did Elijah place on Elisha before being taken up to heaven in a fiery chariot?

9. What miraculous feat was accomplished by both Elijah and Elisha?

10. What animals attacked the children who made fun of Elisha's bald head?

11. When the ax head that Elisha's friends were using fell in the water, what did Elisha do to retrieve it?

12. Did Elisha help cure the Syrian army commander Naaman of blindness or leprosy?

13. Did Elisha contaminate or purify the water in Jericho by throwing a bowl of salt into the spring?

14. Centuries before Jesus was born, Isaiah gave a prophetic picture of his death. True or false?

15. Were Isaiah and Jeremiah known as patriarchs or prophets?

8. his coat (or cloak)

9. They each divided the river Jordan so they could cross over it on dry ground.

10. bears (which mauled forty-two of the children)

11. He made it float on the water.

12. leprosy (a disease of the skin)

13. He purified it.

14. true (The prophecy was made in Isaiah 53, 700 years before Jesus' birth.)

15. prophets (people who were called by God to deliver His message)

GENIUS

16. Was Ezekiel or Elijah the prophet who was lifted up by his hair during a vision?

GENIUS

17. In the proverb quoted by Ezekiel, what sour fruit eaten by the fathers sets the children's teeth on edge?

18. Did the prophet Ezekiel or Isaiah say, "He was pierced for our sins...and by his wounds we are healed"?

19. In Jeremiah, what animal was the prophet speaking of when he asked if it could change its spots?

20. What powerful king dreamed of a great statue of gold, silver, bronze, iron, and clay?

21. Was Daniel or Jonah the Old Testament prophet who prayed three times a day?

22. What country did Daniel and his friends live in as captive servants?

23. Did God bless Daniel and his friends with three times or ten times the insight and wisdom of others?

16. Ezekiel (The spirit lifted him between earth and heaven.)

17. sour grapes (God objected to the proverb, saying the one who eats sour grapes should set his own teeth on edge.)

18. Isaiah (prophesying the coming of the Messiah)

19. the leopard

20. King Nebuchadnezzar

21. Daniel

22. Babylon (under King Nebuchadnezzar)

23. ten times (in every matter of wisdom and understanding)

24. What kingdom was ruled by King Nebuchadnezzar?

25. How many figures did King Nebuchadnezzar see in the furnace even though only three men had been tossed in?

26. What ferocious animals did Daniel not fear because of his faith in God?

27. Was Cyrus a king of Persia or Babylon?

28. What is the one and only book of the Bible in which the name of God is not mentioned?

29. Which prophet married an untrustworthy wife named Gomer: Ezekiel, Amos, or Hosea?

30. Which is the shortest book in the Old Testament: Daniel or Obadiah?

Nice

Answers

24. Babylon

25. four (one was like a son of the gods)

26. lions (When Daniel was in the lions' den, God sent an angel to close their mouths.)

27. Persia (During his reign, Cyrus captured Babylon and let the Israelites return to Jerusalem.)

28. the book of Esther

29. Hosea (God commanded his marriage as a symbol of Israel's lack of faith and God's grace.)

30. Obadiah (with only twenty-one verses)

31. Who lived in the belly of a great fish for three days and three nights?

32. What did Jonah do while he was inside the great fish that swallowed him?

33. Did the people of Nineveh react to Jonah's preaching by killing him or turning from their wicked ways?

34. Which creature did God send to eat the vine that Jonah was using for shade: a ladybug or a worm?

GENIUS

35. Are the city of Nineveh and its evil ways described in the book of Micah, Nahum, or Obadiah?

GENIUS

36. Was Bethlehem prophesied as the birthplace of a future ruler by Micah or Isaiah?

37. Why did Queen Esther keep her nationality a secret from the king of Persia?

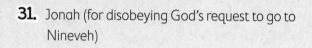

31. Jonah (for disobeying God's request to go to Nineveh)

32. He prayed.

33. They turned from their wicked ways.

34. a worm (God contrasted Jonah's concern about the vine with His concern about Nineveh.)

GENIUS

35. Nahum (who foresees future doom for the city of Nineveh)

GENIUS

36. Micah the prophet

37. because she was Jewish (an Israelite)

GENIUS

38. Who led the Jewish exiles in prayer for forgiveness: Ezra or Ezekiel?

GENIUS

39. Which prophet accused the people of robbing God in tithes and offerings: Nahum or Malachi?

GENIUS

40. Was the rebuilding of the Temple in Jerusalem completed during the reign of King Cyrus or King Darius?

GENIUS

38. Ezra (The exiles acknowledged their sin and committed themselves to God.)

GENIUS

39. Malachi (He encouraged the people to test God's generosity by tithing.)

GENIUS

40. King Darius (who allowed the Temple to be rebuilt according to an earlier decree by King Cyrus)

Jesus' Birth

1. Arrange these books of the New Testament in the proper order: Luke, Matthew, John, Mark.

2. Who is the first person mentioned in the New Testament?

3. The Gospel of Matthew contains no allusions to the Old Testament. True or false?

GENIUS

4. Which two of the four New Testament Gospels mention the birth of Jesus?

5. Were Jesus' parents descended from Samuel or David?

6. What did Zechariah lose because he didn't believe his wife would have a son?

7. Who appeared to Joseph in a dream and told him Mary would give birth to a son named Jesus?

8

Jesus' Birth

1. Matthew, Mark, Luke, John (the first four books of the New Testament)

2. Jesus (in the Gospel of Matthew)

3. false (There are over 125 allusions to the Old Testament in Matthew.)

4. Matthew and Luke (There is no mention of Jesus' birth in Mark or John.)

5. David, the second king of Israel

6. his voice (which he got back after he had written that his son would be named John)

7. an angel (who said the child would be named Jesus because he would save his people from their sins)

GENIUS

8. What was the occupation of Joseph, Mary's husband?

GENIUS

9. What did Elizabeth's unborn baby do when he heard Mary's voice?

10. Before Jesus was born, did Caesar Augustus take a census of Jerusalem or the entire Roman world?

11. Does the Hebrew name Immanuel mean "God is good" or "God is with us"?

12. When Jesus was born, what became his first bed?

13. According to Luke, what did Mary wrap Jesus in before putting him in the manger?

GENIUS

14. Who was told he would not die until he saw the Messiah: Peter, Simeon, or Herod?

15. What heavenly object did the wise men follow to find the baby Jesus?

8. He was a carpenter.

9. He leaped for joy in his mother's womb.

10. the entire Roman world

11. God is with us (according to Matthew 1:23)

12. a manger (where food for the animals was normally kept)

13. swaddling clothes (or strips of cloth)

14. Simeon (who held the eight-day-old Jesus in his arms and was then ready to die in peace)

15. a star (which led the wise men to Bethlehem)

GENIUS

16. Where were Joseph and Mary told to take the baby Jesus to keep him safe from Herod?

GENIUS

17. If people from Samaria were called Samaritans, what were people from Nazareth called?

18. The New Testament covers every year of Jesus' life. True or false?

GENIUS

19. What is the only recorded adventure of Jesus in his boyhood?

16. Egypt (because King Herod wanted to kill Jesus when he heard a new king was born)

17. Nazarenes (Jesus was a Nazarene.)

18. false (There is no reference to Jesus' life between the ages of twelve and thirty.)

19. his visit to the Temple in Jerusalem (without his parents, Mary and Joseph)

9

Jesus' Public Ministry

GENIUS

1. Jesus was baptized in the Sea of Galilee. True or false?

2. Who identified Jesus as the Lamb of God?

3. What bird descended from heaven following the baptism of Jesus?

4. Who was John the Baptist talking about when he said he was unworthy of loosening this man's shoes?

5. To prepare himself for the great task ahead, how long did Jesus stay in the desert?

6. Who said he would give Jesus all the kingdoms of the world if he would bow down to him?

7. How did Jesus begin his verbal response each time the devil tempted him in the desert?

9

Jesus' Public Ministry

GENIUS

1. false (Jesus was baptized in the river Jordan.)

2. John the Baptist

3. a dove (or the Spirit of God as a dove)

4. Jesus (John the Baptist saw Jesus as far superior to himself.)

5. forty days (during which he did not eat and was tempted)

6. Satan (during the third temptation of Jesus in the wilderness)

7. It is written. (Scripture says.)

8. After his three temptations in the wilderness, was Jesus attended by angels, ravens, or lambs?

9. Name two of the four fishermen whom Jesus called to follow him and be his disciples.

10. Who said, "Leave me, Lord, for I am a sinful man"?

11. Fill in the last word of Jesus' promise to his first two disciples: "I will make you fishers of _____."

GENIUS

12. The disciples Peter, Andrew, and Philip all had their homes by the Sea of Galilee. True or false?

GENIUS

13. Which city was NOT on the banks of the Sea of Galilee: Tiberias, Capernaum, or Cana?

14. What type of fishing equipment did Peter, Andrew, James, and John use?

GENIUS

15. Did Jesus meet the woman at the well in Sychar of Samaria or Cana of Galilee?

8. angels (Jesus was exhausted and hungry after fasting and praying for forty days.)

9. Simon (Peter), Andrew, James, and John

10. the Apostle Peter (after catching many fish with Jesus when before he had caught nothing)

11. men (Jesus said these words to Simon and Andrew, who were fishing when he called them.)

GENIUS

12. true

GENIUS

13. Cana (a city near Nazareth and the site of Jesus' first two miracles)

14. fishing nets

GENIUS

15. Sychar of Samaria

GENIUS

16. Did Jesus ask the woman at the well for a drink of water or a place to sleep?

17. During his time in Galilee, did Jesus base his ministry in the city of Capernaum or Nazareth?

18. Did Jesus' hometown of Nazareth reject or adopt his teachings?

19. Besides Peter and Andrew, how many disciples were selected by Jesus?

20. Name one of the two major religious groups that continually opposed Jesus and his teachings.

21. Name the Pharisee who came to Jesus at night and was told he must be born again.

22. Jesus came to abolish the law and the prophets. True or false?

23. Did Jesus upset Jewish leaders by not living in Jerusalem or by healing people on the Sabbath?

GENIUS

16. a drink of water

17. Capernaum (a city on the shore of the Sea of Galilee)

18. Nazareth rejected Jesus' teachings.

19. ten (James, John, Matthew, Philip, Bartholomew, Thomas, another James, Simon, Thaddaeus, Judas)

20. the Pharisees and the Sadducees

21. Nicodemus (a member of the Sanhedrin, the Jewish ruling council)

22. false (Jesus came to fulfill the law and the prophets.)

23. by healing people on the Sabbath

24. Where was Zacchaeus, the tax collector, sitting when Jesus told him to come down immediately?

25. Once some people were so upset with Jesus that they tried to throw him off a cliff. True or false?

26. Which disciple said to Jesus, "You are the Christ, the Son of the living God": Matthew, Philip, or Peter?

GENIUS

27. What two men who had died hundreds of years before appeared with Jesus during his transfiguration?

28. What did Jesus tell the rich young man he must sell to have treasures in heaven?

29. When told he must give up his riches to gain eternal life, did the rich man sell his possessions or walk away?

30. Jesus accused the Pharisees of taxing insignificant things like mint and dill. True or false?

31. Where did the mother of James and John want her sons to sit in the kingdom that Jesus was establishing?

24. in a tree (because he was a short man and wanted to be able to see Jesus over the heads of the crowd)

25. true (the people in the synagogue at Nazareth)

26. Peter (in the Gospel of Matthew)

27. Moses and Elijah (All three appeared before Peter, James, and John.)

28. all his possessions

29. He walked away.

30. true (Jesus said they should pay attention to matters of greater importance.)

31. next to Jesus, on his left and right hand

GENIUS

32. Where were the disciples when they cried to Jesus, "Lord, save us"?

33. Was Bethel or Bethany the home of Lazarus and his sisters Mary and Martha?

34. The Gospel of John contains the shortest verse in the Bible. What two words make up the entire verse?

35. Did the people of Jerusalem cause Jesus great sadness or great joy?

32. in a fishing boat during a storm at sea

33. Bethany (a small village on a slope of the Mount of Olives)

34. Jesus wept. (The verse follows the death of his friend Lazarus.)

35. great sadness (because they killed and stoned prophets)

Jesus' Teaching

1. Are the teachings of Jesus contained mainly in Acts or the Gospels?

2. Complete this verse from the Beatitudes: "Blessed are those who mourn for they will be _____."

3. In the Lord's Prayer, what food should we ask for daily?

4. Where in our house does Jesus say we should go to pray?

5. The Sixth Commandment says "You shall not murder," but what did Jesus say about anger?

6. What creatures did Jesus say do not sow, reap, or gather food into barns?

7. Did Jesus compare Solomon and all his splendor to fruit trees or lilies of the field?

Jesus' Teachings

1. the Gospels (the first four books of the New Testament)

2. comforted (The Beatitudes are part of Jesus' Sermon on the Mount.)

3. (our daily) bread

4. to our room (and shut the door)

5. that we must not even be angry with each other.

6. birds (of the air)

7. lilies of the field (Even Solomon in all his glory was not arrayed like one of these.)

8. Did Jesus say God had numbered his disciples' fingers or the hairs on their head?

9. What do we call the short stories that Jesus used for teaching spiritual truths?

10. In the Bible, who said: "Can the blind lead the blind?"

11. In Jesus' story of a wise man and a foolish man, which one built his house upon a rock?

12. Did Jesus tell his disciples that he sent them out among the wolves as sheep or as chickens?

13. What did Jesus tell his disciples to shake from their feet when people would not listen to their message?

14. In the parable of the rich man who thought he would live many years, what was taken from him that very night?

15. Did Jesus say it was easier for a camel to go through the eye of a needle or for a rich man to go to heaven?

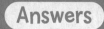

8. the hairs on their head (Jesus was reminding the disciples that their lives were in God's hands.)

9. parables (Jesus tells forty important parables in the New Testament.)

10. Jesus (in his Sermon on the Mount)

11. the wise man (The foolish man built his house on sand.)

12. as sheep (He also said that they should be as wise as serpents and as harmless as doves.)

13. the dust (when they left town)

14. his life (because he stored things for himself and was not rich toward God)

15. for a camel to go through the eye of a needle

16. Whose works did Jesus come to destroy?

17. Did Jesus offer the keys to God's kingdom to Paul, James, or Peter?

18. Did Jesus say adults must become like little children or like little foxes to enter the kingdom of heaven?

19. How many times did Jesus tell Peter we should forgive those who sin against us?

20. In the parable of the Pharisee and the tax collector, who said "Have mercy on me, a sinner"?

21. Before a man builds a tower, does he sit down and figure the cost or does he begin working immediately?

22. What did Jesus say a bad tree produces?

23. In the parable of the net, how will the fishermen divide their catch?

16. the devil's works

17. Peter (Jesus gave him the keys with the words "Upon this rock, I shall build my church.")

18. like little children

19. 490 times (seventy times seven)

20. the tax collector (The Pharisee thought he was better than everyone else.)

21. He sits down and figures the cost (the same way a man figures the cost of becoming a disciple).

22. bad fruit

23. They will keep the good fish and throw away the bad.

24. In the story of the rich man and the beggar Lazarus, which one was carried to Abraham's bosom?

25. After the rich man and the beggar Lazarus died, which one asked to have water put on his tongue?

26. Did Jesus picture the forces of Satan as snakes and scorpions or as lions and tigers?

27. According to Jesus, do evil people prefer the light or the darkness?

28. Does Jesus' story about the persistent friend illustrate the need for continual prayer or continual friendship?

29. Was it the rich man or the Pharisee who said, "Eat, drink and be merry"?

GENIUS

30. What question did Jesus answer in the parable of the Good Samaritan?

GENIUS

31. When he stopped to help the beaten man, was the Good Samaritan on his way to Jerusalem or Jericho?

24. the beggar (The rich man was buried and went to a place of torment called Hades.)

25. the rich man (He was in torment and wanted Lazarus, who was in paradise, to cool his tongue.)

26. as snakes and scorpions

27. the darkness (so they can hide their evil actions)

28. continual prayer (Jesus follows the story with "Ask and it will be given...")

29. the rich man (God called him and that very night the rich man died.)

30. Who is my neighbor?

GENIUS

31. Jericho (from Jerusalem)

GENIUS

32. In the parable of the Good Samaritan, how many men passed by the beaten man and did not help?

33. After the Good Samaritan bandaged the beaten man's wounds, what animal did he place him on?

34. Did Jesus say the "good shepherd" follows his sheep or gives his life for his sheep?

35. Which did Jesus say was the most important of all the commandments?

36. Jesus said we should give everything to God and nothing to Caesar. True or false?

37. In the story of the lost sheep, how many sheep did the shepherd have in all?

38. Which parable tells of a son who left home and wasted all his money?

39. In the parable of the Prodigal Son, who ran down the road to meet the lost son?

32. two (a priest and a Levite)

33. a donkey (to take him to an inn)

34. He gives his life for his sheep.

35. to love the Lord God with all one's heart, soul, and mind

36. false (We should give to God what is God's and give to Caesar what is Caesar's.)

37. one hundred sheep (Even so, the return of one lost sheep to the fold was cause for rejoicing.)

38. the parable of the Prodigal Son

39. his father (who welcomed him home)

40. Did Jesus say his followers would have to take up their cross or their possessions in order to follow him?

GENIUS

41. In the parable of the vineyard and the landowner, did the servants kill the son or honor him with a feast?

42. What did Jesus say a kernel of wheat must do before it grows?

43. In the parable of the king's wedding reception, how many people accepted his invitation?

GENIUS

44. In the parable of the ten talents, what did the wicked servant do with his money?

45. If Jesus is the true "vine," what part of the vine does he call his followers?

46. What amazing feat can be accomplished by a person whose faith is the size of a mustard seed?

40. their cross (Otherwise, they were not worthy of Jesus.)

GENIUS

41. They killed the son (in the hope that they would inherit the vineyard).

42. It must die first.

43. none (They all refused to come.)

GENIUS

44. He hid it in a piece of cloth.

45. the branches

46. That person can move mountains.

47. When the Pharisees wanted to see a miraculous sign, Jesus said the sign of Jonah would be given. True or false?

48. What was Jesus referring to when he said, "Tear down this building and I will rebuild it in three days"?

49. What great day will be like the separating of the sheep from the goats?

50. Did Jesus tell his disciples that he would return as a father arriving home or a thief coming at night?

51. In the parable of the bridesmaids, or virgins, is the lesson to hide your money or always be prepared?

52. What catastrophe did Jesus predict for Jerusalem just before his crucifixion?

53. Who said, "I am the way and the truth and the life"?

47. true (Just as Jonah spent three days in the fish, Jesus would spend three days in the heart of the earth.)

48. his own body (which would die and be resurrected)

49. the day of judgment

50. a thief coming at night (meaning they must be ready for his return at any time)

51. always be prepared (Five of the ten bridesmaids failed to take along enough lamp oil.)

52. Jerusalem and the Temple would be destroyed.

53. Jesus (when the Last Supper had ended)

54. Did Jesus say that within his Father's house there are many rooms or many people?

55. When he was on the cross, to whom did Jesus say, "Here is your mother"?

56. To preach the gospel, did Jesus tell his disciples to go to Jerusalem or out into the world?

54. many rooms

55. John (who took Jesus' mother into his home)

56. out into the world

11

Jesus' Miracles

1. Why did Jesus perform miraculous signs during his ministry?

2. What happened when Jesus told his disciples to toss the fishing net over the right side of the boat?

3. In Jesus' first miracle, did he heal a blind man or change water into wine?

4. Did Jesus cure the son or the daughter of a nobleman who lived in Capernaum?

5. Was it a Roman centurion or an Egyptian judge who believed Jesus could heal his servant from a distance?

6. Who said to the paralyzed man, "Get up, pick up your bed, and go home"?

7. Name the two foods that Jesus used to feed the crowd of five thousand beside the Sea of Galilee.

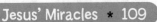

11

Jesus' Miracles

1. so people would know he was the Son of God (and have new life through him)

2. They caught a large quantity of fish (so great that they could not pull the net into the boat).

3. He changed water into wine (at a wedding in Cana).

4. the son (to show the people that he cared)

5. a Roman centurion (Jesus had not found such great faith in all of Israel.)

6. Jesus (after he cured him)

7. bread (loaves) and fishes

GENIUS

8. After Jesus fed the five thousand, how many baskets of leftover food were gathered?

9. After Jesus fed the five thousand, did the crowds want to go home with him or make him their king?

10. Which disciple attempted to go to Jesus by walking on the water?

GENIUS

11. How did Jesus cure the madman in the land of the Gadarenes?

12. Many people believed they would be healed of illness if they could just touch Jesus' clothes. True or false?

GENIUS

13. Of the ten men whom Jesus healed of leprosy all at once, how many returned to thank him?

14. Jesus healed a blind man in Bethsaida by putting saliva on his eyes and putting his hands on him. True or false?

15. When did the disciples say of Jesus, "Even the wind and the waves obey him"?

GENIUS

8. twelve baskets

9. make him their king (Knowing this, Jesus withdrew again into the hills by himself.)

10. Peter (Jesus reached out his hand and kept him from sinking when he grew afraid.)

GENIUS

11. Jesus commanded the madman's demons to enter the bodies of pigs.

12. true (Yet Jesus said it was their faith that would heal them.)

GENIUS

13. only one (a Samaritan)

14. true (The healed man said, "I see people and they look like trees walking around.")

15. When they were all in a tossing boat and Jesus calmed the storm.

16. What did the disciples think they were seeing when Jesus walked toward them on the water?

17. What did Jesus say was the reason that the disciples could not heal a sick boy?

GENIUS

18. What did Jesus tell Peter he would find in a fish's mouth to pay the temple tax?

19. What happened when Jesus put mud on the eyes of a blind man?

20. In Nain, what did Jesus do for a widow at the funeral procession for her son?

21. Who brought Lazarus back to life after he had been dead for four days?

16. a ghost (which frightened them)

17. They had too little faith.

GENIUS

18. a coin (enough to pay the tax for Jesus and Peter)

19. The man was healed and could see again.

20. He brought her son back to life.

21. Jesus (Lazarus and his two sisters were close friends of Jesus.)

Jesus' Final Week

1. What city did Jesus enter on the day that came to be known as Palm Sunday?

2. What animal did Jesus ride into Jerusalem on Sunday of Passover week?

3. Who drove the money changers out of the Temple?

4. How many people joined Jesus for the Last Supper in the upper room?

5. Did Jesus wash his disciples' feet at the Last Supper or on Good Friday?

6. Which disciple said to Jesus, "I will never deny or disown you"?

7. How much money did the priests offer Judas Iscariot to betray Jesus?

Jesus' Final Week

1. Jerusalem (The people of the city covered the road with their cloaks and palm branches.)

2. a young donkey (to show that he came in peace)

3. Jesus (He said the money changers had turned the Temple into a den of thieves.)

4. twelve (Jesus' disciples)

5. at the Last Supper

6. Peter (after the Last Supper)

7. thirty pieces of silver (or silver coins)

8. Jesus did not know ahead of time that Judas Iscariot would betray him. True or false?

9. Name the garden where Jesus was taken into custody.

10. How did Judas Iscariot identify Jesus for the soldiers who came to arrest him?

11. When Jesus was arrested, did the disciples support him or run away from him?

12. Who was the governor of Jerusalem when Jesus was arrested there?

13. Which disciple denied Jesus three times before the rooster crowed at dawn?

14. According to Matthew, did Judas Iscariot die of natural causes or by hanging himself?

15. At the trial of Jesus, what notorious thief did the crowd ask to be released in his place?

8. false (Jesus did know.)

9. the Garden of Gethsemane (where Jesus had gone to pray)

10. He kissed Jesus (so the soldiers would know which one he was).

11. They ran away from him (as Jesus said they would).

12. Pontius Pilate

13. Peter (when Jesus was brought before the Sanhedrin at the house of Caiaphas, the high priest)

14. by hanging himself (In Acts, he falls headlong into a field and his body bursts open.)

15. Barabbas (Pilate freed him and turned Jesus over to the guards.)

16. After Jesus' trial, who asked the question: "What crime has he committed?"

17. After questioning Jesus, Pontius Pilate said: "I find this man guilty." True or false?

18. What kind of crown did the Roman soldiers make for Jesus' head?

19. Was Jesus crucified outside the city of Jerusalem or Bethlehem?

20. How many criminals were crucified alongside Jesus?

21. After the soldiers nailed Jesus to the cross, which of his possessions did they gamble for?

GENIUS

22. During the crucifixion of Jesus, at what time was there complete darkness upon the earth?

23. Did Jesus pray for his enemies or his friends while being put to death on the cross?

16. Pontius Pilate

17. false (Pilate stated: "I find no guilt in this man.")

18. a crown of thorns (ridiculing him as the King of the Jews)

19. Jerusalem (on a hill beyond the city walls)

20. two (one on his right, the other on his left)

21. his cloak, or robe

22. from twelve noon until three P.M. (The sixth hour was twelve noon by ancient time.)

23. his enemies

GENIUS

24. Which were the last words spoken by Jesus from the cross: "I thirst" or "It is finished"?

25. Who asked Pontius Pilate for the body of Jesus?

26. Name two of the four women who arrived at the tomb to anoint Jesus' crucified body.

27. What religious holiday celebrates the resurrection of Jesus?

28. Where were Cleopas and his companion headed when Jesus appeared to them after his resurrection?

29. After his resurrection, how did Jesus get into the locked room where the disciples had hidden?

30. Name the doubting disciple who refused to believe that Jesus was raised from the dead.

31. To convince Thomas of his resurrection, where did Jesus tell him to put his hand?

24. "It is finished." (Immediately after saying these words, Jesus died.)

GENIUS

25. Joseph of Arimathea (who, with Nicodemus, prepared Jesus' body for burial after the Sabbath)

26. Mary Magdalene, Mary (the mother of James), Salome, and Joanna

27. Easter (celebrated at different times in the spring by Christians around the world)

GENIUS

28. to Emmaus (When the travelers recognized Jesus, he disappeared from their sight.)

29. Jesus just appeared with the disciples (even though the doors were locked).

30. Thomas (often referred to as Doubting Thomas)

31. into the side of Jesus (and into his nail-scarred hands)

GENIUS

32. After the resurrection of Jesus, what food did the disciples give him to eat?

33. After his resurrection, how many times did Jesus ask Peter if he loved him?

GENIUS

34. After his resurrection, how many days did Jesus stay on earth before he ascended to heaven?

35. Is Jesus' return to heaven called the ascension or the resurrection?

36. As Jesus ascended to heaven in a cloud, who suddenly appeared next to the disciples on the ground?

37. Who was sent by Jesus to take his place after he left the earth?

Answers

GENIUS

32. (broiled) fish

33. three times

GENIUS

34. forty days (during which time he appeared to the apostles to show he was alive)

35. the ascension (Jesus' return to life is called the resurrection.)

36. two men dressed in white (or angels)

37. the Holy Spirit

13

The Church Is Born

1. Which New Testament book tells about the beginning of the church and the early Christians?

2. Which appeared on the apostles' heads on the Day of Pentecost: tongues of fire or doves of peace?

3. Who gave the sermon on the day of Pentecost?

4. How many people became Christians following Peter's sermon on the day of Pentecost?

5. Did Philip baptize an official from Ethiopia or Samaria?

6. Did Stephen's last speech before the Sanhedrin save his life or cause his death?

7. Who watched the stoning of Stephen: Saul of Tarsus or Judas Iscariot?

The Church Is Born

1. Acts (of the Apostles), probably written by Luke

2. tongues of fire

3. Peter (before tens of thousands from different countries and regions)

4. about three thousand

5. Ethiopia (The official is often referred to as the Ethiopian eunuch.)

6. It caused his death. (In response to his speech, Stephen was stoned to death.)

7. Saul of Tarsus (later known as the Apostle Paul)

8. Who explained to the apostles in Jerusalem that Paul was really a disciple of Jesus?

9. Which apostle was saved from death by being lowered over a wall in a basket?

10. What was the name of the Apostle Paul before it was changed?

11. What blinded Paul on the road to Damascus?

12. After the Christian church grew in Jerusalem and Judea, did it spread next to Samaria or Antioch?

13. Which apostle dreamed of a sheet filled with animals coming down from heaven?

GENIUS

14. Who was so overjoyed to hear Peter at the gate that she forgot to open the door?

GENIUS

15. During the early years of the church, did Agabus prophesy a great flood or a great famine?

8. Barnabas (who became Paul's missionary companion)

9. Paul (His pursuers wanted to kill him for preaching about Jesus.)

10. Saul (His name was changed to Paul after his conversion.)

11. a bright light from heaven (Paul was on his way to Damascus to arrest the followers of Jesus.)

12. Samaria (and then on to the ends of the earth)

13. the Apostle Peter

GENIUS

14. Rhoda (when Peter appeared at the gate after his escape from jail)

GENIUS

15. a great famine (over the entire Roman world)

16. Were Paul and Barnabas sent out as missionaries from the church of Antioch or Jerusalem?

17. When Elymas the sorcerer opposed Paul's message, did God put him in jail or strike him blind?

18. Who deserted the Apostle Paul on one of his missionary journeys?

19. How many missionary trips did the Apostle Paul make?

20. Besides being a missionary and an apostle, how did Paul spend his time?

21. Which apostle was stoned and left for dead in Lystra?

22. Who brought Tabitha (or Dorcas) back to life?

23. Name the husband and wife who made tents while helping Paul when he was at Corinth.

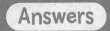

16. the church of Antioch (Paul and Barnabas were the first Christian missionaries of the church.)

17. God struck him blind. (Elymas did not see the sun for a season.)

18. Mark

19. three (In his travels, Paul helped to build up the early church.)

20. He was a tentmaker.

21. the Apostle Paul

22. Peter (He prayed and then turned to her, saying, "Tabitha, arise.")

23. Aquila and Priscilla (Paul, who was also a tentmaker, stayed and worked with them.)

24. What was Luke's occupation in addition to his missionary work?

25. Did Demetrius, who opposed Paul, manufacture souvenirs of Ephesus or silver statues of a goddess?

GENIUS

26. Did the man who appeared in the Apostle Paul's dream invite him to come to Macedonia or Thessalonica?

27. Were Paul and Silas found singing and praying in jail in Philippi or Thyatira?

GENIUS

28. Was Paul in Athens or in Corinth when he read a sign that said "To an unknown god"?

29. When some of the sorcerers in Ephesus became Christians, what did they do to their scrolls?

30. Which is sharper than a double-edged sword: the word of God or a friend's promise?

31. Why were Christians told to put on the full armor of God?

24. He was a doctor (according to Colossians 4:17).

25. silver statues of a goddess

GENIUS

26. Macedonia (a kingdom in ancient Greece)

27. Philippi (a city in Macedonia)

GENIUS

28. in Athens

29. They burned them in a public place.

30. the word of God (according to Hebrews 4:12)

31. to stand against the evils of the devil

32. Did the Apostle Paul compare false teachers to wolves or to lions?

33. Complete this statement: "It is more blessed to give than to _____."

34. Who was tried before Felix, Festus, and King Agrippa?

GENIUS

35. Did Paul heal the chief official and many other people on the island of Malta, Cyprus, or Crete?

36. According to the New Testament, what is a root of all evil?

37. In what city did the Apostle Paul spend two years as a prisoner?

38. What catastrophe occurred as Paul was sailing for Rome to be brought before Caesar?

GENIUS

39. Was it Herod or Agrippa who asked Paul, "Do you think you can persuade me to be a Christian?"

32. to wolves (in sheep's clothing)

33. receive (Paul quotes Jesus' words in his farewell to the Ephesian elders.)

34. the Apostle Paul (in defense of charges brought against him as a troublemaker)

GENIUS

35. Malta (when he was shipwrecked on his way to Rome)

36. the love of money

37. Rome (for preaching against certain Jewish beliefs)

38. a shipwreck (Paul and the other passengers swam to land.)

GENIUS

39. Agrippa (before whom the Apostle Paul pleaded his defense)

40. Which man was a slave who became a Christian while Paul was in jail: Onesimus or Demas?

41. Which is the shortest book in the New Testament?

42. What can separate us from the love of God?

43. According to 1 Peter, who prowls around like a roaring lion?

GENIUS

44. Which is the only New Testament epistle addressed to a woman?

45. Was the Apostle John exiled to the island of Crete or Patmos?

46. When Jesus returns, what instrument will the angels blow to announce his coming?

47. What did Jesus mean when he said, "I am the Alpha and Omega"?

40. Onesimus (Paul speaks on his behalf in his epistle to Philemon.)

41. the second epistle of John (with fourteen verses)

42. nothing (according to Romans 8)

43. the devil (looking for someone to devour)

GENIUS

44. the second epistle of John

45. Patmos (where he wrote the book of Revelation)

46. trumpets

47. I am the beginning and the end. (Alpha and omega are the first and the last letters of the Greek alphabet.)

48. In which prophetic book of the Bible do we read, "Worthy is the Lamb who was slain"?

49. What large, monstrous animal is a symbol of Satan in Revelation?

50. In Revelation 19, Jesus is depicted as an army commander. Is he sitting on a white horse or a black horse?

51. What animal is Jesus compared to most often in the book of Revelation?

48. the book of Revelation

49. the dragon

50. a white horse

51. the lamb

14

Word Power

1. Is "benediction" another word for a blessing, a greeting, or a sacrifice?

2. Is "covenant" a biblical word for a contract or a prayer?

3. Is a menorah a candelabrum, a gemstone, or a kind of tree?

4. In the Bible, is a personal letter called an epistle or an apostle?

5. How many years make a millennium?

6. Which word means "beginnings": genesis or exodus?

7. Is Zion another name for Jerusalem, Jericho, or Joppa?

Word Power

1. a blessing (usually by a minister or priest at the end of a service)

2. a contract (In the Old Testament, God made covenants with Noah, Abraham, Moses, and David.)

GENIUS

3. a candelabrum (A seven-branched menorah stood in the Temple in Jerusalem.)

4. an epistle (An apostle helps to spread the teachings of Jesus.)

5. one thousand years

GENIUS

6. genesis (An exodus is the departure of many people at once from a particular place.)

7. Jerusalem (also called the City of David)

8. The Bible often mentions fasting. What does "fasting" mean?

GENIUS

9. What do we call the special feast that celebrates God's deliverance of the Israelites from Egypt?

10. Was a centurion a Roman military officer or an Egyptian slave?

11. John the Baptist called the religious leaders who came to be baptized a brood of vipers. What are vipers?

GENIUS

12. In the New Testament, is "mammon" another word for bread, water, or wealth?

13. Does the word "testament" refer to a contest or an agreement?

14. Which is another word for a tomb: tabernacle, sepulcher, or synagogue?

GENIUS

15. What biblical figure is sometimes referred to as Beelzebub?

8. abstaining from food (while focusing on God through prayer)

GENIUS

9. the Passover feast

10. a Roman military officer (who had responsibility for a hundred soldiers)

11. poisonous snakes

GENIUS

12. wealth (One cannot serve both God and mammon.)

13. an agreement

14. sepulcher (The tomb where Jesus was buried is sometimes referred to as a holy sepulcher.)

GENIUS

15. Satan (or the devil)

16. What do we call an area in the desert with a source of water?

17. In the Bible, is a cubit used to measure length or weight?

GENIUS

18. The word "amen" means that a prayer is finished. True or false?

16. an oasis (found among trees and plants that grow in the desert)

17. length (A cubit equals about eighteen inches.)

GENIUS

18. false (It signifies agreement with what has been said.)

Miscellaneous

1. Does the Bible compare a person's life span to a spreading tree or a flower that fades?

2. Was the ancient city of Babylon located on the river Nile or the river Euphrates?

3. A dog was a highly desired family pet in biblical times. True or false?

4. Do the terms "rose of Sharon" and "lily of the valley" occur in the Gospels or in the Song of Songs?

5. What bird symbolizes the Holy Spirit?

6. What important crop of biblical times was grown in a vineyard?

7. Grasshoppers were a food in biblical times. True or false?

Miscellaneous

1. a flower that fades

2. the river Euphrates (The site of Babylon is near the city of Baghdad.)

3. false (Dogs were considered lowly animals and usually were not kept as pets.)

4. the Song of Songs (often referred to as the Song of Solomon)

5. the dove

6. grapes (which were eaten fresh, dried as raisins, and used for wine)

7. true (Locusts were also commonly eaten.)

8. About how long did it take to make the seventy-mile trip from Nazareth to Bethlehem by donkey?

9. Did the Israelites use olive oil or wine in their anointing ceremonies?

GENIUS

10. Was it the Pharisees or the Sadducees who did not believe in the resurrection from the dead?

11. Humans judge each other by outward appearances. Where does God look to make his judgment?

12. Which biblical kingdom has no boundaries?

13. Does Jesus sit at the right hand or the left hand of the Father?

14. Samson, David, and Daniel each killed a lion. True or false?

15. What does the bread or cracker represent in the Lord's Supper?

GENIUS

8. three days

9. olive oil

10. the Sadducees

11. at the heart

12. the kingdom of heaven

13. at the right hand of the Father

14. false (Daniel did not have to fight or kill the lions in the den.)

15. the body of Jesus (The Lord's Supper is the Holy Communion.)

GENIUS

16. In Roman times, what was the highest Jewish governing council?

GENIUS

17. How many appearances of the resurrected Jesus are recorded in the Bible?

18. Was Corinth a region in ancient Greece, Egypt, or Persia?

19. In the book of Revelation, is Jesus referred to as the Lion of Judah or the Tiger of Nazareth?

20. Which will last forever: the earth we live on or the word of the Lord?

21. Did the Apostle Paul come from Tarsus, Nazareth, or Rome?

22. In biblical times, what tree was an extremely valuable source of oil?

23. Is Lucifer another name for Luke or for Satan?

16. the Sanhedrin (Jesus, Peter, John, Stephen, and Paul all appeared before this body.)

17. eleven appearances

18. Greece (The Apostle Paul wrote two epistles to the Corinthians.)

19. the Lion of Judah

20. the word of the Lord

21. Tarsus (The life of Paul is detailed in the book of Acts.)

22. the olive tree (The oil was used for many purposes, including oil lamps.)

23. for Satan (the source of all sin and evil)

24. What will God wipe away from our eyes?

25. The river Jordan flows through the Sea of Galilee. True or false?

26. Where are the twelve pearl gates?

27. What animal became the symbol and sign for the early Christians?

28. What part of the ram was used as both a trumpet and an oil container?

29. Was the Old Testament written primarily in Hebrew, Greek, or Latin?

30. Which is NOT a fruit: figs, grapes, olives, manna?

31. In the books of Daniel and Revelation, does the leopard symbolize a peaceful nation or a warring nation?

24. our tears (when we are in heaven)

25. true (The Jordan starts at Mount Hermon and ends in the Dead Sea.)

26. in heaven (the city of heaven)

27. the fish (or sign of the fish)

28. its horn (A ram is a male sheep.)

29. Hebrew (called "the language of Canaan" in the Old Testament)

30. manna (a type of bread)

31. a warring nation

32. What does the cup of grape juice or wine represent in the Lord's Supper?

33. How did God give us the Bible?

34. Which plague was one of the most severe evils that could befall an ancient nation: locusts or ants?

GENIUS

35. How many of the sixty-six books in the Bible belong to the New Testament?

36. Was the tabernacle or the Temple bigger in size and more beautiful in design?

37. The Dead Sea is referred to in the Old Testament as the "salt sea": True or false?

GENIUS

38. Were Jerusalem and the Temple completely destroyed by the Romans in AD 50, 70, or 100?

39. The Bible says we can get to heaven by being good and doing good deeds. True or false?

32. the blood of Jesus Christ

33. God inspired men and prompted them to write.

34. locusts (The devastation of farmland by locusts was regarded as the judgment of God.)

GENIUS

35. twenty-seven books

36. the Temple (The tabernacle was a portable tent for worship.)

37. true (in Genesis 14:3 and Numbers 34:3, to mention two instances)

GENIUS

38. AD 70 (on orders from Titus, the future Roman emperor)

39. false (Only by God's grace and our faith can we get to heaven.)

40. How many major divisions are there in the Bible?

41. Is the Old Testament longer or shorter than the New Testament?

GENIUS

42. In ancient times, Egypt and Israel used cucumbers and melons as part of their regular food. True or false?

43. What is each book of the Bible divided into for easy reference?

44. It took approximately 4,000 years to complete the writing of the entire Bible. True or false?

45. In biblical times, which unit of money had a higher value: a talent or a shekel?

GENIUS

46. How many books in the Bible begin with the letter "Z"?

Answers

40. two (the Old Testament and the New Testament)

41. longer (The Old testament comprises thirty-nine of the sixty-six books in the Bible.)

GENIUS

42. true (Onions and garlic were also common foods.)

43. chapters and verses

44. false (It took approximately 1,500 years.)

45. a talent (The Hebrew silver talent equaled about 3,000 shekels in silver.)

GENIUS

46. two (the books of Zechariah and Zephaniah)